What to doodle?

DINOSAURS!

Chuck Whelon

DOVER PUBLICATIONS, INC.
Mineola, New York

Note

Dinosaurs capture everyone's imagination, and in this unique book you will have a chance to use *your* imagination to create dozens of your own dinosaur scenes. There's plenty of space in each of the sixty-two pictures to add details—just grab a pencil, crayons, or markers and get ready to have some prehistoric fun!

Bibliographical Note

What to Doodle? Dinosaurs! is a new work, first published by
Dover Publications, Inc., in 2010.

International Standard Book Number

ISBN-13: 978-0-486-47514-1
ISBN-10: 0-486-47514-X

Manufactured in the United States by Courier Corporation
47514X03
www.doverpublications.com

What is this T-Rex chasing? Draw it!

1

The paleontologist [someone who studies life forms of prehistoric times] is trying to put these bones together. It's up to you to draw the dinosaur skeleton.

A Parasaurolophus has lost the other dinosaurs in its herd. Draw them in the picture.

Draw the big dinosaur that has frightened this small Compsognathus.

What do you think the Pterodactyl has caught? Draw it.

Draw the fierce opponent that this Triceratops is facing!

Add a pattern to the Dimetrodon's spiny "sail" running along its back.

This gas station owner is dreaming of the dinosaurs that once roamed the desert. Draw a couple of them. (Don't wake him up!)

8

What is this Plesiosaur hunting? Draw its picture.

What dinosaur might have lived in this swampy landscape? Add it to the scene.

Draw a dangerous foe for this well-armored Ankylosaurus.

Provide a creature for this prehistoric person to ride.

A Woolly Mammoth had two enormous tusks.
Add them to this enormous creature.

Draw some long, sharp teeth for this ferocious Sabre Tooth Tiger.

Add some "armor" plates and spikes to the
back of this Kentrosaurus.

On this page, and the page opposite, draw the dinosaurs that are terrorizing the people of this city.

What is the Iguanodon trying to eat in the tree?
Draw a picture of this tasty treat.

Add to this scene the dinosaur that the nest of eggs belongs to.

Draw and decorate a magnificent neck frill for this Chasmosaurus.

The X-ray machine shows what the Giganotosaurus had for lunch. Draw a picture of this meal!

The huge Brachiosaurus wishes that it had some interesting markings on its body. It's up to you to draw some!

Here's your chance to draw a picture of what you think caused the extinction of the dinosaurs.

A Troodon had feathers on its body. Draw what you think they might have looked like.

This Euoplocephalus needs some armor plating. Your task is to draw it.

The paleontologist has discovered a new dinosaur.
Decide what it looks like and draw its picture.

What type of habitat do you think this strange-looking dinosaur might have lived in? Show it.

Here is a herd of long-necked Diplodocus.
Finish drawing their heads and necks.

The duck-billed Hadrosaur had a crest on the top of its head. Add one to the creature below.

**Uh-oh! The volcano is about to erupt!
Add smoke and lava to the scene.**

Draw the creature that is emerging from the sea to walk on land.

Add to this picture the ammonite—an ancient sea creature—that lived in this shell.

The Allosaurus had markings on its face that made it look fierce.
Draw what you imagine these markings may have looked like.

In prehistoric times, many insects were much larger than they are today. Draw some of these awesome creatures!

Add the star attraction to this picture of the Dino Zoo.

What dinosaur would make a good pet? Draw it here!

Some of the earliest creatures might have lived near hot underwater vents like these. Draw some of these tiny sea creatures.

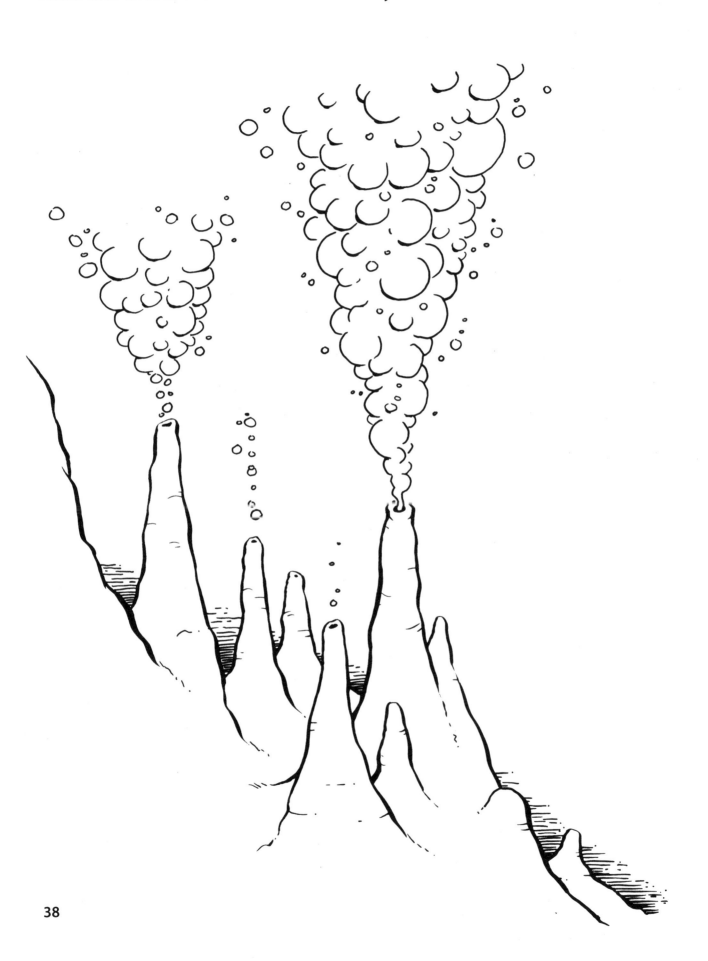

Draw the leader of this group of menacing Deinonychus.

The mother Maiasaura is feeding her babies. How many of them can you draw in this scene?

Add details to the feathers of the birdlike Archaeopteryx.

Finish the picture to show what the Dimorphodon is flying over.

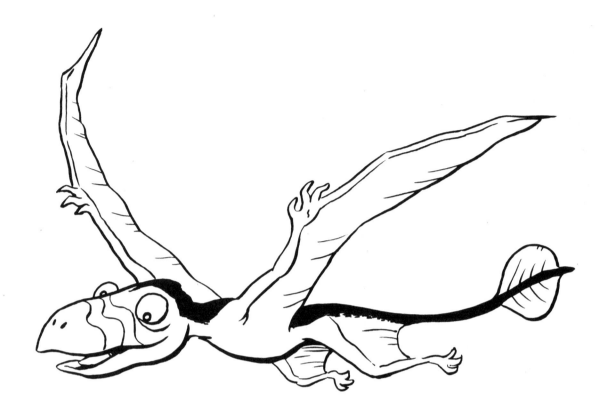

Add spines along the back of this Spinosaurus.

Quetzalcoatlus was a gigantic, toothless flying creature. Draw its massive wings.

What is this Ichthyosaur carrying in its mouth? Draw it—and don't forget to add some sharp teeth to this early marine reptile.

Draw the dinosaur that you imagine this tail belongs to.

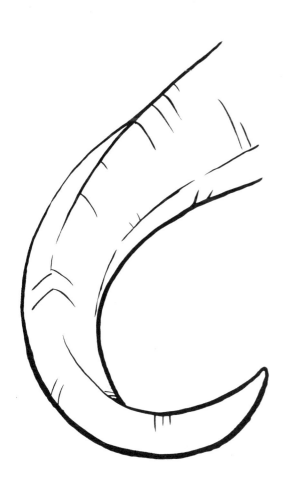

A dinosaur wants to steal the Oviraptor's eggs. Finish the picture.

Draw the dinosaur that is feeding on these tasty prehistoric plants.

What is the Baryonyx about to catch in the water? Draw it!

Add some more horns to the head of this scary Carnotaurus.

**Stenonychosaurus was one of the "smartest" dinosaurs.
What intelligent thing is this one doing? Draw it.**

What sort of scales might this early ancestor of the crocodile have had? Add them to the picture.

Show what the Pachycephalosaurus is charging at with its hard, domed head.

Cryolophosaurus had a fanlike crest on its head. Add some colorful markings to its crest and to the rest of its body.

Therizinosaurus had huge claws—can you draw them?
Add some spines to its back, too!

Draw some large, triangular-shaped bony plates on the back of this Stegosaurus.

What is this pack of Velociraptors attacking? Finish the picture.

The place where this Protoceratops lived was made up of lakes, streams, and plants during the rainy season. Draw this habitat.

The Utahraptor had a crest made of spiky feathers on its head. Add the crest to the picture.

Add a gigantic dinosaur to this scene.

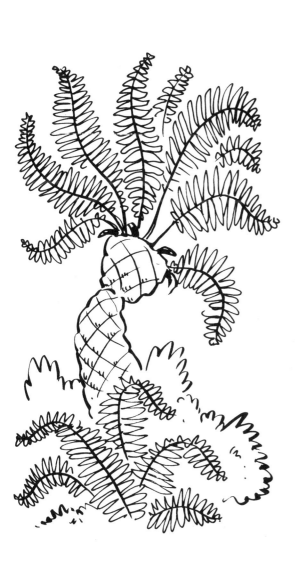

The Struthiomimus is trying to decide what to eat.
Draw in some fruit trees, so it can have its meal.